i

Table of Contents

Executive Summary

The discovery of antibiotics in the early 20th century fundamentally transformed human and veterinary medicine. Antibiotics now save millions of lives each year in the United States and around the world. The rise of antibiotic-resistant bacterial strains, however, represents a serious threat to public health and the economy. The Centers for Disease Control and Prevention (CDC) estimates that annually, at least two million illnesses and 23,000 deaths are caused by antibiotic-resistant bacteria in the United States alone.[1] If the effectiveness of antibiotics (drugs that kill or inhibit the growth of bacteria) is lost, we will no longer be able to reliably and rapidly treat bacterial infections, including bacterial pneumonias, foodborne illnesses, and healthcare-associated infections. As more strains of bacteria become resistant to an ever-larger number of antibiotics, our drug choices have become increasingly limited and more expensive and, in some cases, nonexistent. In a world with few effective antibiotics, modern medical advances such as surgery, transplants, and chemotherapy may no longer be viable due to the threat of infection.

The *National Strategy for Combating Antibiotic Resistant Bacteria* identifies priorities and coordinates investments: to prevent, detect, and control outbreaks of resistant pathogens recognized by CDC as urgent or serious threats, including carbapenem-resistant *Enterobacteriaceae* (CRE), methicillin-resistant *Staphylococcus aureus* (MRSA), ceftriaxone-resistant *Neisseria gonorrhoeae*, and *Clostridium difficile,* which is naturally resistant to many drugs used to treat other infections and proliferates following administration of antibiotics (Table 1); to ensure continued availability of effective therapies for the treatment of bacterial infections; and to detect and control newly resistant bacteria that emerge in humans or animals. This *National Strategy* is the basis of a 2014 Executive Order on Combating Antibiotic Resistance, as well as a forthcoming *National Action Plan* that directs Federal agencies to accelerate our response to this growing threat to the nation's health and security. The *National Action Plan* will be informed by a report approved by the President's Council of Advisors on Science and Technology (PCAST) on July 11, 2014.

The *National Strategy* outlines five interrelated goals for action by the United States Government in collaboration with partners in healthcare, public health, veterinary medicine, agriculture, food safety, and academic, Federal, and industrial research. The goals include:

1. **Slow the Emergence of Resistant Bacteria and Prevent the Spread of Resistant Infections.** Judicious use of antibiotics in healthcare and agricultural settings is essential to slow the emergence of resistance and extend the useful lifetime of effective antibiotics. Antibiotics are a precious resource, and preserving their usefulness will require cooperation and engagement by healthcare providers, healthcare leaders, pharmaceutical companies, veterinarians, the agricultural industry, and patients. Effective dissemination of information to the public is critical. Prevention of resistance

---

[1] Centers for Disease Control and Prevention. *Antibiotic Resistance Threats in the United States, 2013* (http://www.cdc.gov/drugresistance/threat-report-2013/)

also requires rapid detection and control of outbreaks, along with regional efforts to control transmission across community and healthcare settings.

2. **Strengthen National One-Health Surveillance Efforts to Combat Resistance.** Antibiotic resistance can arise in bacterial pathogens affecting humans, animals, and the environment. Strengthening detection and control of resistance requires the adoption of a "One-Health" approach that promotes integration of public health and veterinary disease, food, and environmental surveillance. Improved detection can be achieved through appropriate data sharing, enhancement, expansion, and coordination of existing surveillance systems, and creation of a regional laboratory network that provides a standardized platform for resistance testing and advanced capacity for genetic characterization of bacteria including whole genome sequencing.

3. **Advance Development and Use of Rapid and Innovative Diagnostic Tests for Identification and Characterization of Resistant Bacteria.** Today, researchers are taking advantage of new technologies to develop rapid "point-of-need" tests that can be used during a healthcare visit to distinguish between viral and bacterial infections and identify bacterial drug susceptibilities—an innovation that could significantly reduce unnecessary antibiotic use. The availability of new rapid diagnostic tests, combined with ongoing use of culture-based assays to identify new resistance mechanisms, will advance the detection and control of resistant bacteria, including the priority pathogens listed in Table 1.

4. **Accelerate Basic and Applied Research and Development for New Antibiotics, Other Therapeutics, and Vaccines.** Antibiotics that lose their effectiveness for treating human disease through antibiotic resistance must be replaced with new drugs. Alternatives to antibiotics are also needed in agriculture and veterinary medicine. The advancement of drug development requires intensified efforts to boost basic scientific research, facilitate clinical trials of new antibiotics, attract greater private investment, and increase the number of antibiotic drug candidates in the drug-development pipeline. We must also promote the development of other tools to combat resistance, including new and next-generation antibiotics, vaccines, additional therapeutics, and diagnostics.

5. **Improve International Collaboration and Capacities for Antibiotic Resistance Prevention, Surveillance, Control, and Antibiotic Research and Development.** Recognized by G8 Science Ministers in 2013 as "a major health security challenge of the 21st century," antibiotic resistance is a global problem that requires global solutions. The United States will work in concert with the World Health Organization (WHO), the Food and Agriculture Organization of the United Nations (FAO), the World Organization for Animal Health (OIE), ministries of health and agriculture, and other domestic and international stakeholders to strengthen national and international capacities to detect, monitor, analyze, report and characterize antibiotic resistance; provide resources and incentives to spur the development of therapeutics and diagnostics for use in humans and animals; and strengthen regional networks and global partnerships that help prevent and control the emergence and spread of resistance. The United States will support the development of the WHO *Global Action Plan* to address antimicrobial resistance, strengthen cooperation under the European Union-United States Trans-Atlantic Task Force on Antimicrobial Resistance, promote antibiotic resistance as an international

health priority, and mobilize resources for global activities through multilateral venues such as the Global Health Security Agenda.

Taken together, implementation of specific objectives provided under each goal (Table 2) will help reduce the incidence of the priority pathogens listed in Table 1. National targets for reducing serious and urgent threats by 2020 are provided in Table 3.

Introduction

"Every day we don't act to better protect antibiotics will make it harder and more expensive to address drug resistance in the future. Drug resistance can undermine both our ability to fight infectious diseases and much of modern medicine. Patients undergoing chemotherapy for cancer, dialysis for renal failure, and increasingly common treatments for diseases such as arthritis depend on antibiotics so common infectious complications can be treated effectively."

– Dr. Tom Frieden, MD, MPH, Director U.S. Centers for Disease Control and Prevention

The discovery of antibiotics in the early 20th century fundamentally transformed human and veterinary medicine. Antibiotics now save millions of lives each year in the United States and around the world. The rise of antibiotic-resistant bacterial strains, however, represents a serious threat to public health and the economy. The CDC estimates that annually at least two million illnesses and 23,000 deaths are caused by antibiotic-resistant bacteria in the United States alone.[1]

As more strains of bacteria become resistant to an ever-larger number of antibiotics, our drug choices will become increasingly limited and expensive and, in some cases, nonexistent. If this trend continues unchecked, a wide range of modern medical procedures, from basic dental care to organ transplants, likely would be accompanied by a much greater risk of developing a difficult-to-treat or untreatable antibiotic infection. The safety of many modern medical procedures is dependent on the ability to treat bacterial infections that can arise as post-treatment complications.

Scope of the *National Strategy:* "Antibiotic resistance" results from mutations or acquisition of new genes in bacteria that reduce or eliminate the effectiveness of antibiotics. "Antimicrobial resistance" is a broader term that encompasses resistance to drugs to treat infections caused by many different types of pathogens, including bacteria, viruses (e.g., influenza and the human immunodeficiency virus (HIV), parasites (e.g., the parasitic protozoan that causes malaria), and fungi (e.g., *Candida spp.*). While all of these pathogens are dangerous to human health, this *Strategy* focuses on resistance in bacteria that presents a serious or urgent threat to public health.

Guiding Principles

Our approach to combating the emergence and spread of antibiotic resistant bacteria takes into consideration goals and objectives (Table 2) including the following:

- Misuse and over-use of antibiotics in healthcare and food production continue to hasten the development of bacterial drug resistance, leading to loss of efficacy of existing antibiotics;

- Detecting and controlling antibiotic resistance requires the adoption of a "One-Health" approach to disease surveillance that recognizes that resistance can arise in humans, animals, and the environment;

- Implementation of evidence-based infection control practices can prevent the spread of resistant pathogens;

- Interventions are necessary to accelerate private sector investment in the development of therapeutics to treat bacterial infections because current private sector interest in antibiotic development is limited;

- There are opportunities to use innovations and new technologies—including whole-genome sequencing, metagenomics, and bioinformatic approaches—to develop next-generation tools to strengthen human and animal health, including:

  - Point-of-need diagnostic tests to distinguish rapidly between bacterial and viral infections as well as identify bacterial drug susceptibilities

  - New antibiotics and other therapies that provide much needed treatment options for those infected with resistant bacterial strains;

- Antibiotic resistance is a global health problem that requires international attention and collaboration, because bacteria do not recognize borders.

Goals and Objectives

With these principles in mind, the *Strategy* lays out five interrelated goals that guide collaborative action by the U.S. Government in partnership with foreign governments, individuals, and organizations aiming to strengthen healthcare, public health, veterinary medicine, agriculture, food safety, and research and manufacturing. Those goals include:

1. Slow the emergence of resistant bacteria and prevent the spread of resistant infections;

2. Strengthen national One-Health surveillance efforts to combat resistance;

3. Advance development and use of rapid and innovative diagnostic tests for identification and characterization of resistant bacteria;

4. Accelerate basic and applied research and development for new antibiotics, other therapeutics, and vaccines; and

5. Improve international collaboration and capacities for antibiotic-resistance prevention, surveillance, control, and antibiotic research and development

Taken together, implementation of specific objectives provided under each goal will help reduce the incidence of the priority pathogens listed in Table 1. National targets for reducing serious and urgent threats by 2020 are provided in Table 3.

Development and implementation of the *National Strategy* also supports World Health Assembly (WHA) resolution 67.25 (Antimicrobial Resistance), which was endorsed in May 2014 and urges countries to develop and finance national plans and strategies and take urgent action at the national, regional, and local levels to combat resistance. The resolution specifically calls on WHA Member States to develop practical and feasible approaches to extend the lifespan of drugs, strengthen pharmaceutical management systems and laboratory infrastructure, develop effective surveillance systems, and encourage the development of new diagnostics, drugs, and treatment options.

Development of the Strategy

In December 2013, the President directed the National Security Council (NSC) and the Office of Science and Technology Policy (OSTP) to assess the current and growing threat of antibiotic resistance and develop a multi-sectoral plan to combat resistant bacteria. NSC and OSTP established an interagency policy committee to review past and current Federal efforts to address antibiotic resistance. The committee— which included representatives from the Department of Health and Human Services (HHS), the Department of Agriculture (USDA), the Departments of Homeland Security (DHS), State, Defense (DOD), Veterans Affairs (VA), the U.S. Agency for International Development (USAID), and the Environmental Protection Agency (EPA)—suggested practical, evidence-based ways to enhance antibiotic stewardship, strengthen surveillance for antibiotic resistance and use, advance the development of new diagnostics, antibiotics, and novel therapies, and accelerate research and innovation. The results of the review provided the basis for this *National Strategy.*

Partnerships and Implementation

The *National Strategy for Combating Antibiotic-Resistant Bacteria* will be implemented in accordance with a forthcoming *National Action Plan*, which will detail specific steps and milestones for achieving the *Strategy's* goals and objectives along with metrics for measuring progress. The *National Action Plan* will also address recommendations made in the PCAST *Report to the President on Combating Antibiotic Resistance.*

Implementation of the *National Action Plan* will require the sustained, coordinated, and complementary efforts of individuals and groups around the world, including many who will contribute to its development. These include public and private sector partners, healthcare providers, healthcare leaders, veterinarians, agriculture industry leaders, manufacturers, policymakers, and patients. All of us who depend on antibiotics must join in a common effort to detect, stop, and prevent the emergence and spread of resistant bacteria.

GOAL 1:
Slow the Development of Resistant Bacteria and Prevent the Spread of Resistant Infections

The Opportunity

Judicious use of antibiotics is essential to slow the development of resistance, prevent outbreaks of untreatable infections, and extend the useful lifetime of our most urgently needed antibiotics. At the present time, however, one-third to one-half of all antibiotics used in inpatient and outpatient settings are either unnecessary or incorrectly prescribed.[2] The misuse and over-use of antibiotics not only facilitates the emergence of drug-resistant bacteria, but also exposes patients to needless risk for adverse effects.

Fortunately, a growing body of evidence demonstrates that programs dedicated to improving antibiotic use, known as "antibiotic stewardship" programs, can help slow the emergence of resistance while optimizing treatment and minimizing costs. These programs help providers prescribe the right antibiotic for the right amount of time and prevent prescription of antibiotics for non-bacterial infections. It is imperative that such programs become a routine and robust component of healthcare delivery in the United States. To ensure success, improved data collection systems to monitor improvements in antibiotic usage must also be developed (*see also* Goal 2). Antibiotic stewardship is also needed in agricultural settings because bacteria associated with livestock may contribute to the development of resistance to drugs used in humans. In December 2013, the Food and Drug Administration (FDA) issued *Guidance for Industry* (GFI) #213,[3] which outlines voluntary measures to limit use of medically important antibiotics in livestock.

In addition to slowing the emergence of resistance, it is also critical to prevent transmission of bacteria-causing infections that are resistant to treatment across community and healthcare settings. Outbreaks can be prevented through regional efforts to rapidly detect and control infections that are hard to treat, and also through prompt communications regarding the management and transfer of infected patients within and between healthcare facilities. These interventions, which can be implemented nationally, will be supported by enhanced surveillance activities (Goal 2) that facilitate targeting the most important threats (see Table 1).

Objectives

1.1   Implement public health programs and reporting policies that advance antibiotic-resistance prevention and foster antibiotic stewardship in healthcare settings and the community.

---

[2] Centers for Disease Control and Prevention. Antibiotic Resistance Threats in the United States, 2013 (http://www.cdc.gov/drugresistance/threat-report-2013/); and Vital Signs: Improving Antibiotic Use Among Hospitalized Patients. MMWR March 7, 2014 / 63(09); 194-200.
[3] FDA Guidance for Industry #213 may be accessed at: http://www.fda.gov/downloads/animalveterinary/guidancecomplianceenforcement/guidanceforindustry/ucm299624.pdf.

Implementation steps include working with healthcare facilities, community and professional organizations, state and local health departments, and other partners to:

    i.   A. Strengthen antibiotic stewardship in inpatient, outpatient, and long-term care settings by expanding existing programs, developing new ones, and monitoring progress and efficacy.

            B. Strengthen educational programs such as *Get Smart: Know When Antibiotics Work*,[4] which inform physicians, agricultural workers, and members of the public about good antibiotic stewardship.

    ii.   Expand collaborative efforts by groups of healthcare facilities that focus on preventing the spread of antibiotic resistant bacteria that pose a serious threat to public health (see Table 1).

    iii.   Implement annual reporting of antibiotic use in inpatient and outpatient settings and identify geographic variations and/or variations at the provider and/or patient level that can help guide interventions.

    iv.   Develop and pilot new interventions to address geographic, socio-cultural, policy, economic, and clinical drivers of the emergence and spread of antibiotic resistance and misuse or over-use of antibiotics.

    v.   Streamline the regulatory processes for updating and approving antibiotic susceptibility testing devices, as appropriate, so that clinicians receive up-to-date interpretive criteria to guide antibacterial drug selection.

1.2   Eliminate the use of medically important[5] antibiotics for growth promotion in animals and bring other in-feed uses of antibiotics, for treatment and disease control and prevention of disease, under veterinary oversight.

Implementation steps include working with veterinary organizations, producers, producer organizations, the animal feed industry, the veterinary pharmaceutical industry, and other partners to:

    i.   Implement FDA Guidance for Industry #213 to eliminate the use of medically important antibiotics for growth promotion in animals and bring other therapeutic uses of medically important antibiotics under veterinary oversight. FDA should evaluate the adoption of the proposed changes under Guidance #213 during the three-year implementation period and take further action as appropriate.

    ii.   Assess progress toward eliminating the use of medically important antibiotics for growth promotion in food-producing animals through enhanced data collection on antibiotic sales and use.

    iii.   Develop and implement educational outreach efforts to ensure that veterinarians and animal producers receive information and training to support implementation of these changes.

---

[4] Examples of educational programs on antibiotic stewardship include: Get Smart: Know When Antibiotics Work (www.cdc.gov/getsmart); Get Smart for Healthcare (http://www.cdc.gov/getsmart/healthcare/index.html); and Get Smart: Know When Antibiotics Work on the Farm (http://www.cdc.gov/narms/get-smart.html).

[5] http://www.fda.gov/downloads/AnimalVeterinary/GuidanceComplianceEnforcement/GuidanceforIndustry /UCM299624.pdf (p. 5).

iv.   Optimize public awareness about the progress toward eliminating the use of medically important antibiotics for animal growth promotion.

1.3   Identify and implement measures to foster stewardship of antibiotics in animals.

Implementation steps include working with veterinary organizations, animal producer organizations, and other partners to:

i.   Develop, implement, and measure the effectiveness of evidence-based educational outreach to veterinarians and animal producers to advance antibiotic stewardship and judicious use of antibiotics in agricultural settings.

ii.   Foster collaborations and public-private partnerships with public health, pharmaceutical, and agricultural stakeholders to facilitate identification and implementation of interventions (e.g., good husbandry practices) to reduce the spread of antibiotic resistance.

iii.   Identify, develop, and revise key agricultural practices that allow timely and effective implementation of interventions that improve animal health and efficient production.

iv.   Develop appropriate metrics to gauge the success of stewardship efforts and guide their continued evolution and optimization.

Anticipated Outcomes

Federal agencies will meet these objectives in cooperation with the private sector and other stakeholders to meet the following benchmarks by 2020:

- All States, the District of Columbia, and Puerto Rico will have:
    - Implemented antibiotic stewardship activities in human healthcare delivery settings.
    - Established or enhanced regional efforts to reduce transmission of antibiotic-resistant pathogens and improve appropriate antibiotic use in healthcare facilities across the continuum of care (e.g., acute care, long term care, and outpatient care).

- HHS, DOD, and VA will review existing regulations and propose new regulations and other actions, as appropriate, which require hospitals and other inpatient healthcare delivery facilities to implement robust antibiotic stewardship programs that adhere to best practices, such as those defined by the CDC's Core Elements of Hospital Antibiotic Stewardship Programs.[6]

- At least 95% of eligible hospitals will report antibiotic use data to the National Healthcare Safety Network (NHSN).

- Inappropriate inpatient antibiotic use for monitored conditions/agents will be reduced by 20% from 2014 levels.

- Inappropriate outpatient antibiotic use for monitored conditions/agents will be reduced by 50% from 2010 levels.

- Eliminate the use of medically important antibiotics for growth promotion in animals.

---

[6] The CDC's Core Elements of Hospital Antibiotic Stewardship Programs may be accessed at: http://www.cdc.gov/getsmart/healthcare/implementation/core-elements.html.

- Use of medically important antibiotics in food-producing animals will require veterinary oversight.

- Research efforts will generate validated alternatives to traditional uses of antibiotics, such as changes to health and other management practices, to reduce the need for antibiotics for prevention and treatment of animal diseases.

- The Department of Health and Human Service's Agency for Healthcare Research & Quality and CDC will expand its focus on research and evaluation to develop improved methods and approaches for combating antibiotic resistance and conducting antibiotic stewardship.

GOAL 2:
Strengthen National One-Health Surveillance Efforts to Combat Resistance

The Opportunity

Collection and analysis of data on antibiotic resistance is an important component of biosurveillance, the process of "gathering, integrating, interpreting, and communicating essential information related to all-hazards threats or disease activity affecting human, animal, or plant health"[7] to improve outbreak detection and support decision-making. By linking human, animal, and plant health, this definition recognizes the importance of the *One-Health* approach to addressing emerging infectious diseases, an approach that emphasizes that the health of humans is connected to the health of animals and their shared environment.

Improved detection of resistant bacteria can be achieved through enhancements and expansion of existing surveillance systems that monitor resistance in healthcare settings (such as the National Healthcare Safety Network [NHSN]), in agricultural settings (such as the National Antimicrobial Resistance Monitoring System [NARMS]), and across healthcare and community settings (such as the Emerging Infections Program [EIP]). Enhancements include providing incentives for healthcare-facility reporting, advancing automatic capture of electronic data from healthcare facilities and clinical laboratories, including more diverse patient and community venues as reporting sites, and expanding the sampling of bacterial specimens from agricultural settings. Taken together, improvements to NHSN, EIP, and NARMS will enhance detection of emerging threats in humans and animals, speed outbreak response, and identify populations at greatest medical risk. Moreover, experience with NHSN has shown that reporting also leads to better prevention (Goal 1), because hospitals and state and local health departments use NHSN data to guide local action to interrupt the spread of resistant infections.

To be most useful, the data reported to these systems must be accurate and complete. For that reason, laboratories that test (and report on) resistant bacteria should be linked into a regional network that promotes the use of new technologies and diagnostics (see also Goal 3). The regional network will provide a standardized testing and reporting platform for antibiotic resistance, as well as advanced capacity for genetic characterization of bacteria with rare or unknown resistance mechanisms. These laboratories will serve as a resource that helps healthcare facilities and regional prevention programs investigate outbreaks, quantify the magnitude of resistance problems, and promote accurate testing practices at clinical laboratories. The laboratories that participate in the network will also help establish a national specimen repository for resistant bacteria and a national database of their DNA sequences.

Special investments are required to strengthen surveillance for antibiotic resistance among food animals and foods-of-animal-origin. Expanded capacity for testing, reporting, and data-sharing in veterinary and food safety laboratories will ensure early warning of the emergence of resistance in zoonotic and animal pathogens and enable officials to monitor the preventive impact of the FDA *Guidance for Industry* (GFI) #213 (see Goal 1). Efforts to monitor drug

---

[7] See:
http://www.whitehouse.gov/sites/default/files/National_Strategy_for_Biosurveillance_July_2012.pdf.

resistance patterns in food-producing animals, as well as collection of information on antibiotic drugs sold and distributed for use in food-producing animals, can build on or supplement NARMS, which tracks trends related to antibiotic resistance in food-producing animals, retail meats, and humans.

Objectives

2.1 Create a regional laboratory network to strengthen national capacity to detect resistant bacterial strains and create a specimen repository to facilitate development and evaluation of diagnostic tests and treatments.

Implementation steps include working with healthcare facilities, state and local health departments, clinical laboratories, and many other partners to:

i. Create a regional laboratory network that uses standardized testing platforms to:

- Expand the availability of reference testing services.

- Characterize emerging resistance patterns and bacterial strains obtained from outbreaks and other sources.

- Facilitate rapid data analysis and dissemination of information.

ii. Link data generated by the regional laboratory network to:

- Existing public health surveillance networks so that antimicrobial susceptibility testing (AST) data are immediately available to local, state and federal public health authorities as they detect and investigate outbreaks.

- Veterinary diagnostic and food safety laboratory databases and/or surveillance systems, as needed.

iii. Create a repository of resistant bacterial strains and maintain a well curated, reference database that describes the characteristics of these strains. The repository will aid:

- Biotechnology and pharmaceutical companies that develop new antibiotics, therapeutics, and/or design next-generation tests for diagnosis and susceptibility testing.

- Diagnostic test developers and regulatory agencies who evaluate these tests.

- Government facilities, academic labs, and pharmaceutical companies that test antibiotics for clinical effectiveness.

- Researchers, regulators, and others who assess the effectiveness of interventions to prevent resistance.

- As part of these efforts, the Department of Defense will maintain a repository of resistant bacterial strains and, as appropriate, will update procedures for specimen collection, storage, and data-sharing.

iv. Develop and maintain a national sequence database of resistant pathogens.

2.2 Expand and strengthen the national infrastructure for public health surveillance and data reporting and provide incentives for timely reporting of antibiotic resistance and antibiotic use in all healthcare settings.

Implementation steps include working with governmental and non-governmental partners to:

i. Enhance reporting infrastructure and provide incentives for reporting (e.g., requiring reporting of antibiotic resistance data to NHSN as part of the Centers for Medicare and Medicaid [CMS] Hospital Inpatient Quality Reporting Program).

ii. Add electronic reporting of antimicrobial use and resistance data in a standard file format to the Stage 3 Meaningful Use certification program for electronic health record systems.[8]

iii. Expand the activities and scope of the Emerging Infections Program (EIP) to include monitoring additional urgent and serious bacterial threats (see Table 1) and evaluating populations at risk across community and healthcare settings.

2.3 Develop, expand, and maintain capacity in state and Federal veterinary and food safety laboratories to conduct standardized antibiotic susceptibility testing and characterize select zoonotic and animal pathogens.

Implementation steps include working with state and Federal veterinary and food safety laboratories and many other partners to:

i. Expand and maintain laboratory infrastructure for the identification of select zoonotic and animal health pathogens through the implementation of new diagnostic technologies (see also Goal 3).

ii. Accelerate and standardize antibiotic susceptibility testing and bacterial characterization for select zoonotic and animal health pathogens, coordinating with appropriate stakeholder groups.

iii. Enhance communications and identify mechanisms for sharing and reporting antibiotic susceptibility data on select zoonotic and animal health pathogens collected by State and Federal veterinary diagnostic and food safety laboratories. These data should be stored in a centralized repository that can be linked with relevant public health databases, as appropriate, while maintaining source confidentiality.

2.4. Enhance monitoring of antibiotic-resistance patterns, as well as antibiotic sales, usage, and management practices, at multiple points in the production chain from food-animals on-farm, through processing, and retail meat.

Implementation steps include working with veterinary organizations, animal producer organizations, veterinary and food safety laboratories, and other partners to:

i. Enhance surveillance of antibiotic resistance in animal and zoonotic pathogens and commensal organisms by strengthening the National Antimicrobial Resistance Monitoring System (NARMS) and leveraging other field- and laboratory-based surveillance systems.

ii. Enhance collection and reporting of data regarding antibiotic drugs sold and distributed for use in food-producing animals.

iii. Implement voluntary monitoring of antibiotic use and resistance in pre-harvest settings to provide nationally-representative data while maintaining producer confidentiality.

---

[8] Information on the CMS Meaningful Use program is available at: http://www.cms.gov/Regulations-and-Guidance/Legislation/EHRIncentivePrograms/Meaningful_Use.html.

iv.   Collect quantitative data on antibiotic resistance and management practices along various points at pre-harvest, harvest, and processing, in collaboration with producers and other stakeholders and disseminate information as appropriate.

Anticipated Outcomes

In working towards these objectives with private sector and other stakeholders, Federal agencies will aim to meet the following milestones by 2020:

- Establishment of a regional laboratory network that conducts antibiotic susceptibility testing and other testing to identify outbreaks caused by antibiotic-resistant bacteria and to characterize emerging resistance patterns. The regional laboratory network will participate in international efforts to advance public health communications involving drug resistance (e.g., posting early warning alerts and reporting antibiotic resistance results and trends). See also Goal 5.3.

- Creation of a public electronic portal that will make antibiotic use and resistance data from CDC's monitoring systems publicly available, consistent with the Office Of Management and Budget's Open Data Policy (M 13-13).[9] Optimally, the portal should provide a unified, user-friendly database that facilitates integrated analyses of trends and practices at the state and regional levels.

- Creation of incentives for hospital reporting of data on antibiotic use and resistance to the NHSN, using the NHSN Antimicrobial Use and Resistance (AUR) Module[10] or equivalent update to achieve these reporting targets:

  - At least 95% of eligible hospitals report electronically captured antibiotic resistance data to NHSN.

  - 3,400 acute care hospitals using electronic health records that meet certification criteria for NHSN AUR reporting or successor standard as appropriate.

  - DOD and VA hospitals and long-term care facilities will also use electronic health records that meet certification criteria for AUR reporting or successor standard as appropriate.

- At least twenty veterinary diagnostic laboratories in the National Animal Health Laboratory Network and/or the Veterinary Laboratory Investigation and Response Network (Vet-LIRN) will routinely perform antibiotic susceptibility testing of bacterial strains for which standardized testing methods and data-sharing practices have been established.

---

[9] http://www.whitehouse.gov/sites/default/files/omb/memoranda/2013/m-13-13.pdf.
[10] Information on the NHSN Antimicrobial Use and Resistance (AUR) Module is available at: http://www.cdc.gov/nhsn/PDFs/pscManual/11pscAURcurrent.pdf.

GOAL 3:
Advance Development and Use of Rapid and Innovative Diagnostic Tests for Identification and Characterization of Resistant Bacteria

The Opportunity

Improved diagnostics for detection of resistant bacteria and characterization of their resistance patterns will help physicians make optimal treatment decisions and help public health officials take action to prevent and control disease.

Presently, most diagnostic tests take 24 to72 hours from specimen collection to results, with culture-based tests to determine antibiotic susceptibility adding additional days to weeks. Thus, treatment decisions are typically required and made before laboratory results are available. As a consequence, patients may be initially treated with antibiotics when none are needed, prescribed an inappropriate antibiotic, or treated with multiple antibiotics when a single antibiotic would have been effective.

However, the technological landscape is changing at a rapid pace. The current trend is moving towards clinical presentation or point-of-need diagnostic tests suitable for use during a healthcare visit because they require only minutes. In the future, widespread availability of point-of-need tests that rapidly distinguish between viral and bacterial infections will significantly reduce unnecessary antibiotic use. In addition, scientists will use knowledge of microbial genetics and the molecular determinants of antibiotic resistance to develop rapid, inexpensive molecular tests that identify not only an infecting pathogen, but also its antibiotic-resistance profile.

The development of rapid diagnostic tests, combined with ongoing use of culture-based tests to identify and investigate new resistance mechanisms, will greatly advance detection, control, and prevention of such threats as carbapenem-resistant Enterobacteriaceae (CRE), ceftriaxone-resistant N. gonorrhoeae, Methicillin-resistant Staphylococcus aureus (MRSA), and other multidrug-resistant organisms (MDROs) (see Table 1). These tests will help guide outbreak responses, inform efforts to slow the development of resistance (e.g., the Antibiotic Stewardship programs described in Goal 2), and will have profound domestic and global utility.

In addition to supporting research on diagnostics (see Goal 4), the United States Government can help spur development of diagnostics by providing academic and private sector researchers with representative clinical isolates as well as the technical tools to help address issues related to test development and validation, FDA review, and reimbursement.

Objectives

3.1 Develop and approve new diagnostics, including tests that rapidly distinguish between viral and bacterial pathogens and tests that detect antibiotic resistance that can be implemented in a wide range of settings.

United States Government departments and agencies will work with domestic and international partners to develop rapid diagnostic tests that can:

- Identify clinical illnesses that may benefit from treatment with antibiotics.

- Detect invasive bacterial pathogens in blood, cerebrospinal fluid, synovial fluid, and urine.

- Provide information to guide decisions on treatment and control of CRE, *Neisseria gonorrhoeae*, and other multidrug-resistant organisms.

3.2   Expand the availability and use of diagnostics to improve treatment of antibiotic-resistant bacteria, enhance infection control, and facilitate outbreak detection and response in healthcare and community settings.

Anticipated Outcomes

In working toward these objectives with private sector and other stakeholders, Federal agencies will aim to meet the following benchmarks by 2020:

- Development and dissemination of licensed point-of-need diagnostic tests that distinguish between bacterial and viral infections in 20 minutes or less.

- Validation of diagnostic tests in late-stage clinical trials that determine antibiotic resistance profiles of the 18 bacteria of highest concern (Table 1) in 30 minutes or less.

- Development of well-defined reimbursement policies and incentives to encourage routine use of diagnostics in clinical settings to distinguish between bacterial and viral infections and to ascertain the antibiotic susceptibilities of bacteria.

GOAL 4:
Accelerate Basic and Applied Research and Development for New Antibiotics, Other Therapeutics, and Vaccines

The Opportunity

New therapeutics, vaccines, and diagnostics[11] are urgently needed to combat emerging and re-emerging antibiotic-resistant pathogens. In response, the United States Government has accelerated efforts to advance the discovery and development of novel tools to address antibiotic resistance, with special attention to treatment of multidrug-resistant Gram-negative bacteria, such as CRE and *Neisseria gonorrhoeae,* which are of particular concern because of their diverse and rapidly evolving mechanisms of resistance.

Presently, the pipeline of antibiotics in development is inadequate and commercial interest in antibiotic development remains limited. Nevertheless, a cadre of dedicated innovators, many of them supported by Federal funds, are exploring ways to develop new classes of antibiotics as well as new therapies that could potentially replace the use of antibiotics in agriculture and humans. Efforts are focused at identifying and characterizing new drug targets and developing new therapeutic approaches.

Bringing promising antibiotic candidates to market is a major goal of the Biomedical Advanced Research and Development Authority (BARDA), which is working collaboratively with other government agencies to advance innovative research on antibiotic resistance. Examples include hosting research forums to facilitate the creation of public/private partnerships and launching a "biopharmaceutical incubator" that allows academic institutions and start-up companies to explore creative, early-stage research ideas that could lead to development of new antibacterial drugs or therapies.

Objectives

4.1   Conduct research to enhance understanding of environmental factors that facilitate the development of antibiotic resistance and the spread of resistance genes that are common to animals and humans.

Implementation steps include working with academic and industry partners to:

i.   Support basic research to utilize powerful new technologies and approaches including systems biology to advance the study of antibiotic resistance and address the special problems posed by resistant Gram-negative pathogens such as CRE.

ii.   Leverage existing partnerships, such as the Antibacterial Resistance Leadership Group (ARLG), to reduce obstacles faced by drug companies who are developing new antibiotics. For example, ARLG or another public-private partnership might:

–   Help identify human-subjects qualified for enrollment in clinical trials of antibiotics to treat resistant bacterial infections that occur sporadically, episodically, and/or in limited populations.

---

[11] Diagnostics development is also discussed in Goal 2.

- Generate and apply common clinical test protocols to multiple test group of patients while sharing a common control group.

4.2 **Increase research focused on understanding the nature of microbial communities, how antibiotics affect them, and how they can be harnessed to prevent disease.**

4.3 **Intensify research and development of new therapeutics and vaccines, first-in-class drugs, and new combination therapies for treatment of bacterial infections.**

4.4 **Develop non-traditional therapeutics and innovative strategies to minimize outbreaks   caused by resistant bacteria in human and animal populations.**

4.5 **Expand ongoing efforts to provide key data and materials to support the development of promising antibacterial drug candidates.**

4.6 **Enhance opportunities for public-private partnerships to accelerate research on new antibiotics and other tools to combat resistant bacteria.**

4.7 **Create a biopharmaceutical incubator—a consortium of academic, biotechnology and pharmaceutical industry partners—to promote innovation and increase the number of antibiotics in the drug-development pipeline.**

Anticipated Outcomes

In working toward these objectives with private sector and other stakeholders, Federal departments and agencies will aim to meet the following benchmarks by 2020:

- Two programs sponsored by BARDA will file FDA New Drug Applications for a new antibiotic by the end of 2018.

- Antibiotics developed by two other BARDA-sponsored programs will enter Phase III clinical development by the end of 2016.

- Antibiotics developed by DOD's Defense Threat Reduction Agency-sponsored program will submit pre-Emergency Use Authorization package in 2015.

- USDA will develop at least three drug candidates or probiotic treatments as alternatives to antibiotics for promoting growth in animals (see also Goal 1).

- FDA, USDA, CDC, and the National Institutes of Health (NIH) will encourage private-public sector partnerships to support antibiotic research by hosting a series of Round Table talks for experts in food production, agriculture, and public health.

- By the end of 2014, FDA, USDA, DHS, and National Science Foundation (NSF) will work with the National Institute for Mathematical and Biological Synthesis to develop an analytic modeling framework for assessing the relationship between antibiotic use in livestock (measured at the population level) and the development of antibiotic resistance. The framework will include early milestones and metrics for success.

- FDA, USDA, CDC, DOD and NIH will convene a joint summit to evaluate the status of ongoing research into mechanisms of resistance and its spread among zoonotic pathogens and commensal microbiota. The research projects may make use of whole genome sequencing, proteomics, metagenomics, structural biology, and bioinformatics.

- FDA, USDA, CDC, NIH, DOD, and EPA will conduct annual evaluations to ensure that research resources are focused on high-priority resistance issues.

- A mechanism will be in place to ensure that datasets on antibiotic resistance generated through federally funded research, including genomic and proteomic data sets, are publicly available through searchable online databases in a manner that is consistent with protecting personally identifiable information (see also Objective 2.1).

- The gut microbiome of at least one animal species raised for food will be sequenced and characterized to advance our understanding of the structure and function of gastrointestinal microbial communities. This research may help identify new growth promotants, antibacterial interventions that do not disrupt the normal gut intestinal microbiota of food animals, and may provide insight into management of the human microbiome.

GOAL 5:
Improve International Collaboration and Capacities for Antibiotic Resistance Prevention, Surveillance, Control, and Antibiotic Research and Development

The Opportunity

Domestic action alone is insufficient to protect the nation's public and agriculture health and security. Resistance occurs naturally, but careless practices in drug supply and use or overuse — both in the United States and in countries around the world - are rapidly increasing the prevalence of hard-to-treat infections in both animals and humans. Antibiotic resistance represents a major economic burden on healthcare systems as resistant strains of bacteria cost more to treat and often require prolonged treatment. In the worst of cases, a strain is resistant to all of the available drugs and presents a threat to our global health security. The pipeline for new and more effective antibiotics is not well-stocked, and without action, the world may soon lose the easiest way to treat infections and keep people alive and healthy.

Effectively combating antibiotic resistance will require government, industry, academia, and the human and animal health sectors across the globe to work together. The global community is faced with limited tools to address this global threat due to a critical lack of data on the magnitude, epidemiology and economic impact of antibiotic resistance, as well as the paucity of diagnostic and therapeutic options. The actions the United States takes domestically must be complemented by coordinated international action in order to ensure that resistant strains that arise in one part of the world are rapidly detected, diagnosed, and contained at the source of emergence. The United States and international partners must work to promote innovation in drug and diagnostics development, enhance stewardship of existing antibiotics in human and agricultural settings, and strengthen systems for detecting, diagnosing, and monitoring resistance so that reporting is timely, accurate, and transparent.

International momentum for addressing the urgent threat of antibiotic resistance continues to grow at a political level. The United States has supported ongoing exchanges with the European Union through the Trans-Atlantic Taskforce on Antimicrobial Resistance (TATFAR), which was established in 2009 by President Obama and his European counterparts to improve cooperation on combating resistance. TATFAR serves as an effective model for international collaboration on antibiotic resistance both in terms of enabling robust technical exchanges as well as facilitating transparency and identifying best practices. In June 2013, G8 Science Ministers collectively agreed that resistance is a "major health security challenge of the 21st century" and affirmed the pivotal role that science plays in addressing global challenges like drug resistance. Additionally, the recent endorsement of resolution 67.25 by the World Health Assembly has triggered an international, WHO-led process to develop a Global Action Plan for Antimicrobial Resistance. The United States continues vigorously to support this process, which will provide a broad framework that will facilitate coordinated national and global investments to combat resistance. The Global Health Security Agenda (GHSA), launched by the United States in partnership with nearly 30 countries in February 2014, includes preventing and detecting resistance as a key component, and the GHSA will provide an important forum for securing international financial and technical commitments to combat resistance in support of the WHO Global Action Plan.

United States Government agencies will work with ministries of health, agriculture, and food safety, WHO, Food and Animal Organization (FAO), World Organization for Animal Health (OIE), the European Union, and other partners to advance global efforts to combat antibiotic bacteria. Multilateral efforts will include: supporting the development of the WHO Global Action Plan to Address Antimicrobial Resistance; strengthening cooperation under the European Union-United States TATFAR; increasing political awareness regarding the health, economic, and security impacts of antibiotic resistance; and mobilizing broader international support to combat antibiotic resistance through venues such as the recently launched GHSA. As needed and appropriate, United States Government agencies will provide information, technical assistance, and/or capacity-building resources to underdeveloped and developing nations throughout the world.

Objectives

Surveillance: Establish capacity to detect, analyze, and report antibiotic resistance in order to make information needed for evidence-based decision making available in each country and globally.

5.1 **Promote laboratory capability to identify at least three of the seven WHO priority AMR pathogens[12] using standardized, reliable detection assays.**

The WHO AMR Pathogens and types of resistance of concern include:

- *Escherichia coli*: resistance to 3rd generation cephalosporins and to fluoroquinolones

- *Klebsiella pneumoniae*: resistance to 3rd generation cephalosporins and to carbapenems

- *Staphylococcus aureus*: methicillin resistance, or MRSA

- *Streptococcus pneumoniae*: resistance (non-susceptibility) to penicillin

- Non-Typhoidal *Salmonella* (NTS): resistance to fluoroquinolones

- *Shigella* species: resistance to fluoroquinolones

- *Neisseria gonorrhoeae*: reduced susceptibility to 3rd generation cephalosporins

5.2 **Collaborate with WHO, OIE, and other international efforts focused on the development of harmonized, laboratory-based surveillance capacity to detect and monitor antibiotic resistance in relevant animal and foodborne pathogens.**

5.3 **Develop a mechanism for international communication of critical events that may signify new resistance trends with global public and animal health implications.**

5.4 **Promote the generation and dissemination of information needed to effectively address antibiotic resistance by:**

---

[12] The WHO priority AMR pathogens are a subset of the pathogens identified as urgent and serious threats in Table 1.

i. Supporting consistent international standards for determining whether bacteria are resistant to antibiotics.

ii. Developing international collaborations to gather country-specific and regional information on drivers of antibiotic resistance, identify evidence-based interventions and adapt these strategies to new settings, and evaluate their effectiveness.

iii. Provide technical assistance to developing nations to improve their capacity to detect and respond effectively to antibiotic resistance.

Research and Development: Incentivize development of therapeutics and diagnostics for humans and animals.

5.5 **Establish and promote international collaboration and public-private partnerships to incentivize development of new therapeutics to counter antibiotic resistance including new, next-generation, and other alternatives to antibiotics; vaccines; and affordable, rapidly deployable, point-of-need diagnostics.**

Prevention and Control: Strengthen systems in countries, regional networks, and global partnerships to prevent and control the emergence and spread of antibiotic resistance through evidence-based interventions, and monitor and evaluate the effectiveness of those interventions.

5.6 **Support countries to develop and implement national plans to combat antibiotic resistance and strategies to enhance antimicrobial stewardship.**

5.7 **Partner with other nations to promote quality, safety, and efficacy of antibiotics and strengthen their pharmaceutical supply chains.**

5.8 **Coordinate regulatory approaches by collaborating with international organizations such as FAO and OIE to harmonize international data submission requirements and risk assessment guidelines related to the licensure and/or approval of veterinary medicinal products including antibacterial agents, vaccines, and diagnostics to the extent possible.**

Anticipated Outcomes

In working toward these objectives with private sector and other stakeholders, Federal agencies will aim to meet the following benchmarks by 2020:

- Work with at least 30 partner countries to develop surveillance capacity to monitor and slow the rate of increase of antibiotic resistance, including at least one reference laboratory per country capable of identifying at least three of the seven WHO priority AMR pathogens (see page 19) using standardized, reliable detection assays, and reporting these results appropriately.

- Work with international partners to support the development and implementation of the *WHO Global Action Plan for Antimicrobial Resistance (AMR)*.

- Support the development of a secure website or portal for real-time data-sharing among international public health partners on antibiotic-resistant bacteria to facilitate early warning and notification of significant events to WHO, ECDC, and other relevant global public health organizations.

- Develop a common system with the European Union for sharing and analyzing bacterial resistance patterns for the 18 CDC priority pathogens (Table 1), which include the seven WHO priority pathogens.

- Support efforts to harmonize and integrate antibiotic-resistance surveillance data on WHO and CDC priority pathogens generated by WHO regional surveillance networks.

- In collaboration with partner nations and the WHO, FAO, and OIE, explore the establishment of a common mechanism for accelerating investment in research on the development of new and next generation antibiotics, including novel therapeutics, vaccines, and rapid, inexpensive, and rapidly deployable, point-of-care diagnostics; similarly coordinate research on the microbiomes of various species of food animals.

- Forge key partnerships aimed at reducing the use of medically important antibiotics for growth promotion in food animals and strengthening antibiotic stewardship in all human settings.

- Collaborate with other OIE member countries to establish a global database to collect harmonized quantitative data on the use of antibacterial agents in animals.

- Establish a process for international communication of critical events that may signify new resistance trends, including those with global public health implications.

- Work with WHO, FAO, and OIE to build on Codex Alimentarius[13] and other risk-management frameworks to assess country-specific and regional drivers of antibiotic resistance and work with Ministries of Health and Agriculture to adopt interventions that have proven successful in other settings.

---

[13] The Codex Alimentarius is a collection of internationally recognized standards, codes of practice, and guidelines relating to foods, food production, and food safety (http://www.codexalimentarius.org/codex-home/en/).

Next Steps

Over the next six months, an interagency task force co-chaired by the Secretaries of Health and Human Services, Agriculture, and Defense will develop a National Action Plan for Combating Antibiotic-Resistant Bacteria that will detail the specific steps that agencies are taking, or will take, both individually and in coordination to implement this *National Strategy*. The task force will also address recommendations made in a recent report by the President's Council of Advisors on Science and Technology on Combating Antibiotic Resistance. The National Action Plan will establish clear milestones and metrics for success. These activities will be coordinated by the White House National Security Council and Office of Science and Technology Policy. Because this initiative will require a sustained effort, the task force will regularly report to the President on progress made in implementing the National Strategy and Action Plan, and toward achieving the National Targets described in Table 3. It is expected that departments and agencies would also take steps to combat antibiotic resistance that are not explicitly included in either the National Strategy or Action Plan; these efforts will also be included in the progress report to the President. Industry and other non-governmental organizations as well as international partners will play a key role in accelerating progress in combating antibiotic resistance. This *National Strategy* will solidify an ongoing partnership among these entities that will ensure resources are leveraged effectively to address this urgent threat to public health and national security.

The *National Strategy* is intended to promote greater investment and coordination of U.S. Government resources to reduce antibiotic-resistant bacteria, but the *National Strategy* is not a budget document and does not imply approval for any specific action under Executive Order 12866 or the Paperwork Reduction Act. The *National Strategy* will inform the Federal budget and regulatory development processes within the context of the goals articulated in the President's Budget. All activities included in the *National Strategy* are subject to budgetary constraints and other approvals, including the weighing of priorities and available resources by the Administration in formulating its annual budget and by Congress in legislating appropriations.

Table 1:
CDC's Antibiotic-Resistant Threats in the United States, 2013

URGENT Threat Level Pathogens

Clostridium difficile

- 250,000 infections per year requiring hospitalization or affecting hospitalized patients.

- 14,000 deaths per year.

- At least $1 billion in excess medical costs per year.

- *C. difficile* deaths increased 400% between 2000 and 2007 because of the emergence of a strain resistant to a common antibiotic class (fluoroquinolones).

- Almost half of infections occur in people younger than 65, but more than 90% of deaths occur in people 65 and older.

- Half of *C. difficile* infections first show symptoms in hospitalized or recently hospitalized patients, and half show symptoms in nursing-home patients or in people recently cared for in doctors' offices and clinics who received antibiotics.

- The majority (71%) of pediatric *Clostridium difficile* infections, which are bacterial infections that cause severe diarrhea and are potentially life-threatening, occur among children in the general community; 73 % were found to have recently taken antibiotics prescribed in doctor's offices for other outpatient settings.[14]

Carbapenem-Resistant Enterobacteriaceae

- Out of approximately 140,000 healthcare-associated Enterobacteriaceae infections per year, more than 9,000 are caused by CRE (7,900 CR-*Klebsiella* spp; 1,400 CR-*E. coli*).

- Over 600 deaths per year (520 CR-*Klebsiella* spp; 90 CR-*E. coli*).

- 44 states have had at least one type of CRE confirmed by CDC testing.

- CRE are resistant to nearly all antibiotics including carbapenems – an antibiotic of last resort.

Neisseria gonorrhoeae (Notifiable to CDC)

- *Neisseria gonorrhoeae* causes gonorrhea, is the second most common reportable infection in the United States, and is developing resistance to the cephalosporin antibiotics (such as ceftriaxone), the last-line effective treatment option for this infection.

- Of the 820,000 cases per year, 30% (246,000) now demonstrate resistance to at least one antibiotic.

- If ceftriaxone-resistant *N. gonorrhoeae* becomes widespread, the public health impact during a 10-year period is estimated to be 75,000 additional cases of pelvic inflammatory

---

[14] Wendt, J.M. et al. *Clostridium difficile* Infection Among Children Across Diverse US Geographic Locations. Pediatrics. January 3, 2014.

disease, 15,000 cases of epididymitis, and 222 additional HIV infections, with an estimated direct medical cost of at least $235 million.

SERIOUS Threat Level Pathogens

Multidrug-Resistant *Acinetobacter*

- 12,000 healthcare-associated *Acinetobacter* infections occur in the U.S. of which 7,000 are multidrug-resistant.

- ~500 deaths per year

- At least three different classes of antibiotics no longer cure resistant *Acinetobacter* infections.

Drug-Resistant *Campylobacter*

- *Campylobacter* causes ~1.3 Million infections, 13, 000 hospitalizations and 120 deaths each year; 310,000 (25%) drug-resistant *Campylobacter* infections are found each year

- *Campylobacter* drug resistance increased from 13% in 1997 to 25% in 2011.

- *Campylobacter* spreads from animals to people through contaminated food, particularly raw or undercooked chicken and unpasteurized milk.

- Antibiotic use in food animals can and does result in resistant *Campylobacter* that can spread to humans.

Fluconazole-Resistant *Candida*

- Out of 46,000 Candida yeast infections per year, 3,400 (30%) of patients with bloodstream infections with DR-*Candida* die during their hospitalization.

- CDC estimates that each case of *Candida* infection results in 3-13 days of additional hospitalization and a total of $6,000-$29,000 in direct healthcare costs per patient.

Extended Spectrum β-Lactamase (ESBL)-Producing *Enterbacteriaceae*

- Extended spectrum β-lactamase (ESBL) is an enzyme that makes bacteria resistant to a wide spectrum of penicillins and cephalosporins.

- Of 140,000 Enterobacteriaceae infections per year, 26,000 are drug-resistant, causing 1,700 deaths.

- 26,000 healthcare-associated Enterobacteriaceae infections are caused by ESBL-Enterobacteriaceae.

- Enterobacteriaceae infections result in greater than $40,000 excess hospital charges per occurrence.

Vancomycin-Resistant *Enterococcus*

- Of 66,000 *Enterococcus* infections per year, 20,000 are drug-resistant causing 1,300 deaths.

- *Enterococcus* strains resistant to vancomycin have few or no treatment options.

Multidrug-Resistant Pseudomonas aeruginosa

- Of 51,000 *Pseudomonas* infections per year, 6,700 are multidrug-resistant causing 440 deaths.

- 13% of severe healthcare-associated infections caused by *Pseudomonas* are multidrug-resistant, meaning nearly all or all antibiotics no longer cure these infections.

Drug-Resistant Non-Typhoidal *Salmonella* (Notifiable to CDC)

- Non-typhoidal *Salmonella* causes 1.2 million infections per year, of which 100,000 are drug-resistant resulting in 23,000 hospitalizations and 450 deaths each year.

- Non-typhoidal *Salmonella* results in more hospitalizations, longer stays, and higher treatment costs.

Drug-Resistant *Salmonella enterica serovar Typhi* (Notifiable to CDC)

- Of 21.7 M *Salmonella typhi* infections worldwide, 5,700 illnesses in the U.S. with 3,800 (67%) of infections are drug-resistant resulting in 620 hospitalizations each year.

- Before the antibiotic era or in areas where antibiotics are unavailable, 20% of *Salmonella typhi* infections result in death.

Drug-Resistant *Shigella* (Notifiable to CDC)

- *Shigella* causes ~500,000 illnesses, 5,500 hospitalizations, and 40 deaths each year in the U.S.

- Since 2006, *Shigella* resistance to traditional first-line antibiotics has become so high that physicians must now rely on alternative drugs (ciprofloxacin and azithromycin) to treat infections.

Methicillin-Resistant *Staphylococcus aureus* (MRSA)

- Over 80,000 invasive MRSA infections and 11,285 related deaths per year (in 2011).

- Severe MRSA infections most commonly occur during or soon after inpatient medical care.

- Between 2005 and 2001, overall rates of invasive MRSA dropped 31% predominantly due to appropriate medical procedures implemented in central-line maintenance.

Drug-Resistant *Streptococcus pneumoniae* (Notifiable to CDC)

- Of 4 million disease incidents and 22,000 deaths, 1.2 M are drug-resistant [to amoxicillin and azithromycin (Z-Pak)], resulting in 19,000 excess hospitalizations and 7,900 deaths.

- In 30% of *S. pneumoniae* cases, the bacteria are fully resistant to one or more antibiotics, causing complications in treatment and death.

- Pneumococcal pneumonia accounts for 72% of all direct medical costs for treatment of pneumococcal disease and in excess of $96 million in medical costs per year.

- Pneumococcal conjugate vaccine (PCV) prevents disease, reduces antibiotic resistance by blocking the transmission of resistant *S. pneumoniae* strains, and protects against 13 strains of *S. pneumoniae*.

Drug-Resistant *Tuberculosis* (Notifiable to CDC)

- Tuberculosis (TB) is among the most common infectious diseases and cause of death worldwide.

- Of 9,588 TB cases in the U.S. in 2013, it is estimated that 1-2% of these cases were resistant to antibiotics with direct costs for treatment of MDR-TB averaging $134,000 per case (in 2010 dollars)

- CDC funds health departments in all 50 states, 10 large cities, DC, Puerto Rico, the Virgin Islands and other territories to conduct surveillance, provide laboratory testing, perform contact investigations, diagnose cases and provide directly-observed therapy and medical management for TB cases and therapy for latent TB infection. Five TB Regional Training and Medical Consultation Centers (RTMCCs) provide training and medical consultation for these programs.

OF CONCERN Threat Level Pathogens

Vancomycin-Resistant *Staphylococcus aureus* (Notifiable to CDC)

- Few cases, thus far (13 cases in 4 States since 2002).

- Staph *aureus* strains resistant to vancomycin have very few or no treatment options.

Erythromycin-Resistant Group A *Streptococcus*

- Group A Strep (GAS) causes many illnesses, including strep throat (up to 2.6 M cases per year), toxic shock syndrome, and "flesh-eating" disease (necrotizing fasciitis, 25-35% fatal).

- Erythromycin-resistant GAS causes 1,300 illnesses and 160 deaths.

- Current concern is the increase in bacteria that show resistance to clindamycin, which has a unique role in treatment of GAS infections.

Clindamycin-Resistant Group B *Streptococcus*

- Of 27,000 GBS cases, 7,600 illnesses are drug-resistant, resulting in 440 deaths in the United States each year.

Additional information may be found in the CDC report *Antibiotic resistance threats in the United States, 2013* (http://www.cdc.gov/drugresistance/threat-report-2013/).

Table 2:
Goals and Objectives for Combating Antibiotic-Resistant Bacteria

GOAL 1: Slow the Emergence of Resistant Bacteria and Prevent the Spread of Resistant Infections

Objectives

1.1   Implement public health programs and reporting policies that advance antibiotic-resistance prevention and foster antibiotic stewardship in healthcare settings and the community.

1.2   Eliminate the use of medically important antibiotics for growth promotion in animals and bring other in-feed uses of antibiotics, for treatment and disease control and prevention of disease, under veterinary oversight.

1.3   Identify and implement measures to foster stewardship of antibiotics in animals.

Goal 2: Strengthen National One-Health Surveillance Efforts to Combat Resistance

Objectives

2.1   Create a regional laboratory network to strengthen national capacity to detect resistant bacterial strains and a specimen repository to facilitate development and evaluation of diagnostic tests and treatments.

2.2   Expand and strengthen the national infrastructure for public health surveillance and data reporting, and provide incentives for timely reporting of antibiotic resistance and antibiotic use in all healthcare settings.

2.3   Develop, expand, and maintain capacity in State and Federal veterinary and food safety laboratories to conduct standardized antibiotic susceptibility testing and characterize select zoonotic and animal pathogens.

2.4   Enhance monitoring of antibiotic-resistance patterns, as well as antibiotic sales, usage, and management practices, at multiple points in the production chain from food-animals on-farm, through processing, and retail meat.

Goal 3: Advance Development and Use of Rapid and Innovative Diagnostic Tests for Identification and Characterization of Resistant Bacteria

Objectives

3.1 Develop and approve new diagnostics, including tests that rapidly distinguish between viral and bacterial pathogens and tests that detect antibiotic resistance that can be implemented easily in a wide range of settings.

3.2 Expand availability and use of diagnostics to improve treatment of antibiotic-resistant infections, enhance infection control, and facilitate outbreak detection and response in healthcare and community settings.

Goal 4: Accelerate Basic and Applied Research and Development for New Antibiotics, Other Therapeutics, and Vaccines

Objectives

4.1 Conduct research to enhance understanding of ecological determinants and environmental factors that facilitate the development of antibiotic resistance and the spread of resistance genes that are common to animals and humans.

4.2 Increase research focused on understanding the nature of microbial communities, how antibiotics affect them, and how they can be harnessed to prevent disease.

4.3 Intensify research and development of new therapeutics and vaccines, first-in-class drugs, and new combination therapies for treatment of bacterial infections.

4.4 Develop non-traditional therapeutics and innovative strategies to minimize the effects of resistant bacteria in human and animal populations.

4.5 Expand ongoing efforts to provide key data and materials to support the development of promising antibacterial candidates.

4.6 Enhance opportunities for public-private partnerships to accelerate research on new antibiotics and other tools to combat resistant bacteria

4.7 Create a biopharmaceutical incubator—a consortium of academic, biotechnology and pharmaceutical industry partners—to promote innovation and increase the number of antibiotics in the drug-development pipeline

Goal 5: Improve International Collaboration and Capacities for Antibiotic Resistance Prevention, Surveillance, Control, and Antibiotic Research and Development

Objectives

Surveillance for Resistant Bacteria

5.1 **Promote laboratory capability to identify at least 3 of the 7 WHO priority AMR pathogens[15] using standardized, reliable detection assays.**

5.2 **Collaborate with WHO, OIE, and other international efforts focused on the development of harmonized, laboratory-based surveillance capacity to detect and monitor antibiotic resistance in relevant animal and foodborne pathogens.**

5.3 **Develop a mechanism for international communication of critical events that may signify new resistance trends with global public and animal health implications.**

5.4 **Promote the generation and dissemination of information needed to address antibiotic resistance by:**

> **5.4.1** **Promote consistent international standards for determining whether bacteria are resistant to antibiotics; and**
>
> > a) Develop international collaborations to gather country-specific and regional information on drivers of antibiotic resistance, identify evidence-based interventions, adapt these strategies to new settings, and evaluate their effectiveness; and
> > b) Provide technical assistance as needed to underdeveloped and developing nations to improve their capacity to detect and respond effectively to antibiotic resistance.

Research and Development

5.5 **Establish and promote international collaboration and public-private partnerships to incentivize development of new therapeutics to counter antibiotic resistance including new, next-generation, and other alternatives to antibiotics; vaccines; and affordable, rapidly deployable, point-of-need diagnostics.**

Prevention and Control

5.6 **Support countries to develop and implement national plans to combat antibiotic resistance and strategies to enhance antimicrobial stewardship.**

5.7 **Partner with other nations to promote quality, safety, and efficacy of antibiotics and strengthen country pharmaceutical supply chains.**

---

[15] A list of WHO priority AMR pathogens is provided on page 18. These pathogens are a subset of the pathogens identified as Urgent and Serious Threats in Table 1.

5.8   Coordinate regulatory approaches by collaborating with international organizations such as FAO and OIE to harmonize international data submission requirements and risk assessment guidelines related to the licensure and/or approval of veterinary medicinal products including antibiotics, vaccines, and diagnostics, to the extent possible.

Table 3:
National Targets for Combating Antibiotic-Resistant Bacteria

By 2020, the United States will:

For CDC Recognized Urgent Threats:

- Reduce by 50% the incidence of overall *Clostridium difficile* infection compared to estimates from 2011.

- Reduce by 60% carbapenem-resistant Enterobacteriaceae infections acquired during hospitalization compared to estimates from 2011.

- Maintain the prevalence of ceftriaxone-resistant *Neisseria gonorrhoeae* below 2% compared to estimates from 2013.

For CDC Recognized Serious Threats:

- Reduce by 35% multidrug-resistant *Pseudomonas* spp. infections acquired during hospitalization compared to estimates from 2011.

- Reduce by at least 50% overall methicillin-resistant *Staphylococcus aureus* (MRSA) bloodstream infections by 2020 as compared to 2011.*

- Reduce by 25% multidrug-resistant non-typhoidal *Salmonella* infections compared to estimates from 2010—2012.

- Reduce by 15% the number of multidrug-resistant TB infections.

- Reduce by at least 25% the rate of antibiotic-resistant invasive pneumococcal disease among <5 year-olds compared to estimates from 2008.

- Reduce by at least 25% the rate of antibiotic-resistant invasive pneumococcal disease among >65 year-olds compared to estimates from 2008.

* This target is consistent with the reduction goal for MRSA bloodstream infections (BSI) in the *National Action Plan to Prevent Healthcare-Associated Infections (HAI): Road Map to Elimination,* which calls for a 75% decline in MRSA BSI from the 2007-2008 baseline by 2020. Additional information is available at http://www.health.gov/hai/prevent_hai.asp#hai_plan.

www.ingramcontent.com/pod-product-compliance
Lightning Source LLC
Chambersburg PA
CBHW080734290526

45790CB00008B/3183